CREATIVE ADVENTURE GUIDES

Starting a Business:
Have Fun and Make Money

By Carla Mooney

NORWOOD HOUSE PRESS

Norwood House Press
PO Box 316598
Chicago, Illinois 60631

For information regarding Norwood House Press, please visit our Web site at:

www.norwoodhousepress.com or call 866-565-2900.

© 2011 by Norwood House Press.

Picture Credits: AP Images, 6; © B.A.E. Inc./Alamy, 19; © bildagentur-online/begsteiger/Alamy, 18; Bloomberg/Getty Images, 23; Courtesy of Raffi Darrow, 40, 41, 42; © Chad Ehlers/Alamy, 7; © Richard C. Bingham II/Alamy, 9; Getty Images, 15; © imagebroker/Alamy, 31; © Phillip Lewis/Alamy, 16; Courtesy of Jason O'Neill, 37, 38; Joseph Paris, 24; David Sacks/jupiter images, 20; Courtesy of Hayleigh Scott, 4, 8, 34, 35; © Steve Skjold/Alamy, 21; © Tom Stewart/Corbis, cover, 28; Washington Post/Getty Images, 11; © Steven Widoff/Alamy, 12; © WoodtStock/Alamy, 26

LIBRARY OF CONGRESS CATALOGING-IN-PUBLICATION DATA
Mooney, Carla, 1970-
Starting a business : have fun and make money / Carla Mooney.
p. cm. -- (Adventure guides)
Includes bibliographical references and index.
Summary: "A step-by-step guide for developing a business for fun and profit. Includes developing a business plan, conducting market research, developing a budget and banking. Chronicles three children entrepreneurs who have also incorporated philanthropy into their business model. Glossary, additional resources and index"--Provided by publisher.
ISBN-13: 978-1-59953-386-5 (library edition : alk. paper)
ISBN-10: 1-59953-386-3 (library edition : alk. paper)
1. New business enterprises--Juvenile literature. 2. Small business--Juvenile literature. I. Title.
HD62.5.M6656 2010
658.1'1--dc22
.   2010010405

Manufactured in the United States of America in North Mankato, Minnesota.
158N—072010

Table of Contents

Ten-year-old Hayleigh started her own business making hearing aid charms.

4

Chapter 1

Getting Started:
Find Your Idea

Have you ever wanted extra money to buy the latest video game or some new clothes? Maybe you have bigger goals. You want to save for college or a special purchase like a car or flat-screen television. Most people get a job when they want to earn money. For kids under 16, finding a job can be hard. Why not make your own job? You can make money by starting your own business.

Every year thousands of kids go into business for themselves. Some walk dogs or mow lawns. Others bake cookies or design jewelry to sell. These enterprising kids turn something they like doing into a way to earn money. With a little planning, you can start a business too!

What Is an Entrepreneur?

People who start and run their own businesses are called entrepreneurs. Before they start a business, entrepreneurs do their homework. First, they find something that people need. Then they figure out a way to fill that need.

Two famous entrepreneurs are Ben Cohen and Jerry Greenfield. They wanted to sell something everyone eats—ice cream. First, the two friends took an ice cream-making class through the mail. Then in 1978, they opened the first Ben & Jerry's ice cream shop in Vermont. They made their ice cream different by mixing unusual flavors. Ben & Jerry's ice cream quickly became a customer favorite. The pair also thought of creative ways to sell and advertise their products. On their store's first anniversary, they gave out free ice cream. This helped more people find out how good their ice cream tasted. Today Ben & Jerry's stores still celebrate Free Cone Day. Ben and Jerry started their business with one small shop. Today, they sell ice cream in shops and grocery stores across the country.

Ben Cohen (left) and Jerry Greenfield, founders of Ben & Jerry's ice cream, are examples of entrepreneurs.

Types of Businesses

Most businesses are one of three main types. The first type is a service business. These businesses do things for people. Some may walk dogs. Others may clean houses or paint walls. People pay service businesses to do things that they do not want to do. Others pay because they do not have time to do it themselves. Most kids start a service business because it is the easiest business to start. It also costs less to run.

A second type of business is manufacturing. These businesses make and sell products. They could make items like jewelry, cookies, or dog collars. To start, you usually have to buy supplies. This often means the business costs more to start. Still, these businesses can

Kids participate in a car wash. Providing such services can be the basis for a business.

be very **profitable.** Making products can also be good for creative people.

A third type of business is trade or retail. These businesses sell products that other people make. Toys"R"Us is an example of a retail business.

Ten Ideas for Kid Businesses

Here are ten kid business ideas that might help you **brainstorm**:

1. Jewelry maker
2. Dog walker
3. Pet sitter
4. Party helper
5. Tutor
6. Lawn care service
7. Baker
8. Babysitting service
9. Elderly helper
10. Housecleaner

These are some of Hayleigh's hearing aid charms that can also be used as earrings.

Finding an Idea

To find the right business idea for you, think about the following questions:

- What am I good at doing?
- What do I like to do?
- What are my goals?
- Do I want to earn money to buy something special, or do I want to create an ongoing business?
- How much time will I have to spend on the business?

To help you think about these questions, try writing down your talents and interests. Then brainstorm business ideas that match them. The best business uses your talents. It should also be something fun and interesting for you to do.

The more time you put into developing your business idea, the better chance you have of making it succeed.

Tips for Success: Communication

Entrepreneurs deal with people every day. How you communicate can be key to your success. Here are some tips:

- When talking to an adult in person or on the phone, speak up. Do not be afraid or embarrassed to talk.
- Speak slowly and clearly.
- If you call someone and no one answers, do not hang up. Leave a message with your name, phone number, and the reason you called.
- Take notes when talking to someone for your business. This will help you remember important information.
- When someone calls or emails you, always call or email them back within 24 hours if possible.
- When sending business emails, always be polite and professional. Keep your writing free of slang.

Evaluate the Market

You have a list of several possible business ideas. The next step is to **evaluate** the market. A market is the people who will buy your product or service. A business idea might be great, but you need to sell it. If no one wants to buy your product or service, then you will not be very successful.

To evaluate your market, think about these questions:

- Who are the people in your neighborhood who would buy your product or service?
- What needs do the people in your neighborhood have? Does your product or service fill one of those needs?

- Is there a different product or service that you could offer that is a better fit with the people you know?
- Is there someone who already sells the same service or product in your neighborhood? If so, then how can you make yours different or better? Why should people choose you over the **competition**?

If you are having trouble deciding whether your product or service is needed, ask your friends and neighbors. They might be able to give you **feedback** on your business idea.

Thirteen-year-old Taylor Denchfield started his own dog-walking business.

Other Things to Think About

Once you have a business idea, you should consider a few other things. First, will you need help to run your

business? Many kid businesses are small enough that one person can run them alone. Others work better with a partner or an adult's help. For example, if you want to start a dog-walking service, who will walk the dogs when you are sick or on vacation? Maybe you should have a partner or backup person to call. You may also need an adult to drive you or order supplies. Before you start, you should talk to these people to make sure they agree to help you.

Another important item to think about is **start-up costs**. For some businesses, like a lemonade stand or jewelry-making business, you need to buy supplies before you sell a product. Do you have the money to buy these start-up supplies? If not, how do you plan to get it? Maybe you can work extra chores at home to earn the money. You might also be able to ask your parents for a loan. You can promise to pay back the loan as soon as your business starts making money.

Starting a business takes careful thinking and lots of planning. With a little work, you can find the perfect business that fits you.

Chapter 2

Business Basics

To run a business, you need to know some basic business concepts. This knowledge will help you start your business on the right path.

Marketing

Marketing is getting the word out to customers about your business. This includes finding a **target market**, testing it, and **advertising** to it.

A good idea for every business is to find its target market. It is easier to sell to a group of people who are more likely to buy. For example, people who own dogs are more likely to buy dog-walking services than people who have cats. What if you do not know who your target market is? To find out, you can **survey** a group of people. The group should include people of all ages. In the survey, you can ask them questions about your business. See if they would buy your product or service. For a lawn care business, you might find out that your target market is couples who are too busy to mow their lawns. Once you find your target market, you should focus all your sales efforts on it.

Advertising is another key part of marketing. Businesses advertise so that people will know who they are and what they do. One easy way to advertise is to make and hand out flyers and business cards. You can give them to your neighbors. You can also post them at town halls, libraries, schools, and churches. Before you post a flyer in a public place, make sure you ask for permission. Some businesses create a special **logo**. A logo helps people remember a business. Everyone knows the swoosh on Nike sneakers, for example. You can make your own logo on a computer and add it to your marketing.

Advertising your business, as these kids are doing for their car wash, is another important aspect to starting your own business.

Publicity is another good way to tell people about your business. Local newspapers and magazines often like to run stories about kids in business. You can contact your local papers and see if they would like to write an article about your business. That way many people

Lawn care is a good idea for a business, but deciding whose equipment you will use and how much you will charge are decisions you should make before you start.

in your community can learn about your business.

Some people buy radio or newspaper ads to tell people about their business. Others offer coupons or have special sales.

Pricing

One important decision is how much money you will charge for your product or service. It should be priced high enough that you can make money. On the other hand, you do not want your prices to be too high. In fact, lower prices tend to attract more customers.

Before you set your price, find out what your competition charges. Look into similar businesses run by kids and adults. For example, an adult lawn care service might charge 50 dollars per mowing. A local teenager charges 30 per cut. You might want to set your price even lower, around 25 dollars per mowing. The lower price may get customers to take a chance on your new business. As you gain experience, you can raise your prices.

Bank Accounts

Most businesses open a bank account for their money. You might already have your own bank account. Opening a different account for your business is a good idea, though. That way you can keep the business's money separate from your own money. As a bonus, most banks will pay **interest** on the money in your bank account.

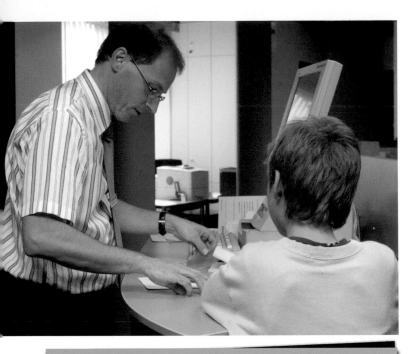

Enlisting your parents to help you open a bank account and attend to other financial concerns can be a good idea.

may want to open a savings account. A savings account will pay you more interest.

Every month the bank will send you a statement. The bank statement lists all of the **deposits**, checks cashed, and interest earned on your account during the month. It also shows your **account balance**. The bank might also send a copy of your cancelled or cashed checks.

Profit

How does a business know if it is making money? Profit is the money a business expects to have. You figure out profit with this simple formula: **income** – **expenses** = profit. A business's income is the money it makes from selling. Expenses are payments a

The type of bank account you open depends on your needs. If you write checks to pay for supplies, you might need to open a checking account. If you do not need to write checks, you

Tips for Success: Making a Budget

Many business owners use a budget to help them plan their business. A budget is an estimate of how much income a business expects to earn and the expenses they expect to pay in a period. A period can be a month, quarter of a year, or year. To make a budget for your business, follow these steps:

1. Write down everything you plan to sell. Estimate and write down how much money you think you will make from each item.
2. Write down all of the expenses that you think your business will have. Estimate and write down how much you think you will spend during each period.
3. Calculate your budget profit. Remember, income – expenses = profit. If your profit is zero or negative, you need to think about your income and expenses. Is there a way you can increase your income? Could you raise prices or sell more items? Is there a way to cut back on your expenses?
4. The final step of working with a budget is comparing it to your actual sales and expenses. See where your estimates were right and where you were wrong. This can help you make a better budget the next time. Comparing your budget to your actual results tells you other things too. You might learn where you need to cut costs, what items are selling well, and if your prices are high enough.

Keeping expenses as low as possible helps to make your profit higher.

Selling items that you no longer need and items from friends and family can be the start of an ongoing garage sale business. Since you already own the items, it can be more profitable than other businesses.

business makes. You may pay to buy supplies or pay someone who helped you. Most businesses figure out their profit on a regular basis. That may be every week, month, or quarter. Knowing if you are making or losing money is important. It can show you if there are problems in your business. If you are not making money, you may need to increase your prices. You may also need to cut back on expenses.

Record Keeping

Good record keeping is an important part of every business. Records hold lots of information. Customer lists tell a business who buys from it. **Supplier** lists show the best places to buy supplies. Sales records show income. Payment records show expenses. Some businesses keep records of how much time people spend working. Businesses also keep records to show their **accounts receivable** and **accounts payable**.

When you sell a product, record what it was and the amount you collected for it. You can keep this record in a notebook or computer file. When you buy something, keep the receipt in an expense file. Then record it on an expense work sheet. You can look at these records to see which items are selling well. You can also see which items are not selling well.

A young man keeps track of the finances from his business on a computer. Using accounting software like this can help keep finances organized.

Most businesses keep their records in files. You can store electronic files

Tips for Success: Negotiating

Negotiation is the way you discuss and work out an agreement. You can negotiate with customers, suppliers, and employees. If you are working for someone else, you may also negotiate how much he or she pays you.

Before you start, you should know what you want. Make sure you clearly ask for it. For example, you may plan to charge five dollars per walk for your dog-walking service. You should tell your potential customers up front. Sometimes they might agree to your price. Other times they may try to negotiate or change the terms. Maybe they only want to pay four dollars per walk. When you are negotiating, make sure you listen to the other person's point of view. You might hear a clue that will help you give them what they want. You might not need to lower your price. Instead, offer something extra such as a weekly dog brushing. This may help you negotiate successfully without giving up what you want.

on a computer. You can also use envelopes or file folders to keep paper records. The most important part is to keep the files organized. That way you can easily find the information when you need it.

Taxes

Every business pays some of its profit to the government. This is called paying taxes. If your business makes more than a few hundred dollars, it will probably have to pay taxes. There are federal, state, and local taxes. Every area has different rules about taxes. You can research tax rules for your community on the Internet. You can usually get tax forms from local libraries, post offices, or Web sites.

Paying a portion of your profits in taxes is something all business owners must do.

It is a good idea to ask an adult for help with your business taxes. Not paying your taxes or paying the wrong amount can get you in serious trouble with the government. Even if you are a kid, you could be fined!

Now that you know some business basics, you are ready to plan the details for your own business.

Chapter 3

Writing Your Own Business Plan

Tommy's Fresh Lemonade Business Plan

When they start a business, many entrepreneurs write a business plan. A business plan is exactly what it sounds like—a plan to run the business. Writing the plan helps the entrepreneur think about all the details they will need to know for their business.

A business plan describes the business. The plan includes information about the market and answers several questions. Who will buy products or services? Who will run the business? How will they run it? What are the advertising plans? Does anyone else sell the same products or service? How is this business better or different than others?

Most business plans also include an estimate of how much money the entrepreneur thinks the business will make.

Now that you have an idea for a business, you can write a business plan too. The steps on the following pages will show you how to write a plan for a sample business, a lemonade stand.

Who will buy products or services?

How much money will the business make?

Who will run the business?

How is this business better?

Section One: Description

The first section of your business plan describes the business. It should say your business name and describe your product or service. It will also include where you will make and sell your products or services.

> A good business plan, like the one below, is important to make clear to yourself and others what you intend to accomplish.

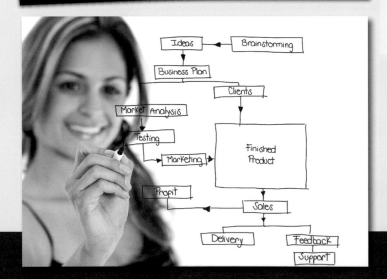

Example: Tommy's Fresh Lemonade will open on June 1, 2009. It will sell homemade lemonade made with real lemons. Customers can buy the lemonade in three sizes: small, medium, and large. Tommy's will also sell homemade chocolate chip cookies. Customers can buy single cookies or by the dozen. During the summer months—June, July, and August—Tommy's will be located in a booth outside the Treesdale Community Pool. During the school year—September through May—Tommy's will be closed.

Section Two: Market Analysis

In this section of your plan, you will describe the overall market for your business. Why is it a good market to get into? What needs are not being met? Who is your target market? This is also a good section to describe your ideal customer. Researching this information will help you target your sales efforts. This means you can spend your time selling to the people most likely to buy.

Example: Swimmers and families from several neighborhoods come to the Treesdale Community Pool. Most people at the pool are families with young children and teenagers. The pool's snack stand does not sell lemonade or cookies. They only sell soda, chips, and ice cream. Some people, especially children, do not like the fizzy taste of soda. Tommy's Fresh Lemonade will meet this need by selling lemonade and cookies at the pool. A Tommy's customer will be a child who asks his or her parent for a drink and cookie.

Section Three: Competition

This section describes your competitors. Competitors are people who sell the same product or service as you. Compare your product or service with theirs. How are they different? Think about why yours is better. What can you do to make yours stand out from the competition? If theirs is better, how can you improve your product?

Example: The pool snack stand is the main competition for Tommy's Fresh Lemonade. It also sells drinks and snacks to people at the pool. It does not offer the same choices. The pool snack stand only sells soda. Tommy's stands out because it offers things—lemonade and cookies—that the snack stand does not have.

If other businesses in your neighborhood provide a similar service to yours, what can you offer that's different or better?

Section Four: Marketing

In this section, you will describe how you plan to market your business. Think about how you will get people to buy your product or service. What type of advertising will you do? Also, think about how much you will charge for your product or service.

Example: Tommy's Fresh Lemonade has a big sign and stand that attract attention near the pool's entrance. In addition, Tommy has made flyers. He will pass them out to homes in the local neighborhood. He will also hand out flyers to people as they enter and leave the pool. Tommy's will get additional publicity from the local newspaper. It will be running an interview with Tommy in an article about what kids do in the summer.

Tips for Success: Being Polite

Have you ever heard the phrase "The customer is always right"? This means that people in business should always be polite to their customers, even if the customers are being rude to them. When a customer argues with you or complains about your business, remember to use your best manners. Try your best to listen to the complaints. See if there is a way to help the customer as much as you can. Sometimes a customer may be unreasonable. In that case, it is a good idea to excuse yourself politely. Try to talk to them later when they have calmed down.

Section Five: Management

In this section you will write about who is going to run the business. Are you going to run everything by yourself? If not, will you need help from a partner or an adult? If you need people to help you run the business, you need to think about how you will pay them.

Example: Tommy's Fresh Lemonade is run alone by Tommy. He performs all tasks and selling. At times, Tommy's mother will help at no charge by driving him to the store to buy supplies. She will also help with tax and banking paperwork.

Tips for Success: Safety

It is important to be safe when running your business. Some good safety practices include the following:

- Check with your parents before emailing someone you do not know.
- Do not give out personal information over the phone.
- Be careful giving business or personal information to anyone you do not already know and trust.
- Never go alone to someone's house if you do not know him or her. Bring a parent the first time.
- Make sure you tell your parents where you are going to be, what you are doing, and when you expect to be home.

Section Six: Operations

In this section, you need to discuss how you plan to run your business. Where will it be located? When will you work on it? Talk about how you plan to make your product or provide your services. You should also list the supplies that you will need here.

Example: Tommy's Fresh Lemonade will be located at a stand near the Treesdale Community Pool. It will only be open on days when the pool is open in June, July, and August. The stand will open at 12:00 noon and sell until 3:00 P.M. Because Tommy's house is next door to the pool, he will make the lemonade and bake the cookies in his kitchen in the morning. Then he will bring them to the stand. If he needs more lemonade or ice, he can quickly get them from his house.

Make a list of the supplies you will need so you can plan out costs.

To make the lemonade, Tommy will use his grandmother's recipe for fresh-squeezed lemonade. He will use lemons, sugar, water, and ice. For the cookies, Tommy plans to use another family recipe. He will need sugar, flour, chocolate chips, butter, eggs, vanilla, and baking soda. The business will also need lemonade pitchers and cookie sheets. Tommy will also have to buy cups and napkins for the customers.

Tips for Success: Naming Your Business

Picking a name for your business is an important decision. A business's name should clearly tell people what it does. When choosing a name, you should try to make sure you do not copy another business's name. Check the names of other businesses by looking in phone books and doing Internet searches. Some state Web sites even have a page that lets you search business names. After you have picked your name, you can register it with your state to make sure no one else uses your name. The rules for registering a business name are different in each state. In some states, you may have to pay a fee. You can check your state's Web site to get more information.

Section Seven: Budget

In this section, you will need to create a budget for your business. You should estimate how much you will sell in a certain period. Your budget will have all the income you expect to earn. It should also list the expenses you expect to pay. Your budget will predict if your business is going to make a profit. If there's no profit, you may need to change your prices or cut some expenses.

For the budget at right, Tommy plans to have his stand open for 20 days in June. He thinks that he will sell 20 glasses of lemonade each day at 50 cents per glass. His budgeted lemonade income is $200 (20x20x$0.50). Tommy also thinks he will sell 10 cookies each day at 25 cents per cookie. His budgeted cookie income is $50 (20x10x$0.25).

Example:

Tommy's Fresh Lemonade	
Budget: June 2009	
Income:	
Sales: Lemonade	$200
Sales: Cookies	$50
Total Income	$250
Expenses:	
Lemons	$30
Sugar	$20
Baking Supplies	$20
Cups	$10
Napkins	$10
Total Expenses	$90
Net Profit	**$160**

Hayleigh proudly displays the charms she makes for her business.

Chapter 4

Making It Work:
Real Kids in Business

Lots of kids become entrepreneurs. Here are three success stories of kids who have turned something they like to do into a business.

Hayleigh's Cherished Charms

Ten-year-old Hayleigh is the founder of Hayleigh's Cherished Charms. Her business makes and sells decorative charms for hearing aids. Hayleigh was born with a hearing impairment. As a young child, she attended a school for the hearing impaired. There Hayleigh noticed that many of the kids hid their hearing aids behind their hair. She felt that instead of

Hayleigh's business idea—making charms to decorate hearing aids—came from her real-life experience.

hiding them, the kids should be proud of their hearing aids. She began to draw pictures of jewelry to decorate the hearing aids. She decided to take her drawings and turn them into a business.

Hayleigh makes her charms in a special work area at home. She can make a charm in less than ten minutes. Hayleigh buys supplies for the charms at a local craft store or orders them online. She has made more than 50 different charm designs. Some charms include Swarovski crystals. Others are dogs, cats, or holiday-themed with penguins and trees. All of her charms can also be made into earrings for people who wear only one hearing aid or do not wear any hearing aids.

To market her charms, Hayleigh wears them to school and when she goes out with her family. She has also put up charm displays in **audiologist** offices. Hayleigh passes out business cards to people she meets. She has even launched a Web site for her business.

Tips for Success: Contracts

A contract puts an agreement that a business makes into writing. The agreement can be with a customer, supplier, or other person. Having a contract helps if you disagree with another person about the agreement. It proves in writing what was agreed upon.

Good contracts should include:

- the names and signatures of people involved
- the date the contract is signed
- a description of what each person agrees to do and when he or she will do it
- payment terms—price, when due, and who will pay

With the money she makes from her business, Hayleigh is saving for college. She also donates 10 percent of her profits to schools for the deaf and hearing research. In the future Hayleigh hopes to open her own store. She says that she sees herself doing this for her whole life. For kids who are considering starting a business, Hayleigh has a few tips. First, it should be something that they want to spend time doing. Second, Hayleigh says to remember that if you're frustrated, just know that you should just keep going and never give up!

Pencil Bugs

When Jason was nine years old, he asked his mother if he could help her make something for a craft fair. When

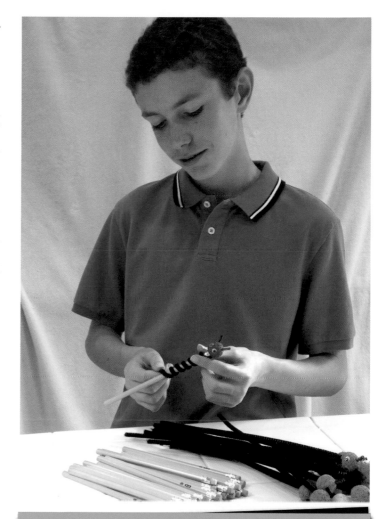

Jason's idea for his business started out as a whim.

After his initial success, Jason realized his Pencil Bugs could become a full-fledged business.

toppers that he called Pencil Bugs. His first batch of 24 Pencil Bugs sold out at the craft fair. Jason then made a few more with his extra supplies and took them to school. When kids began to ask him to make some for them, he realized he had a business.

Jason researched how to start a business online. To get the word out about Pencil Bugs, Jason held several sidewalk and craft fair sales. Word of mouth quickly spread about Jason's Pencil Bugs. Within a few months, his mom created a Web site for his business. Jason also uses Twitter and Facebook to market his business online. In addition, he has gotten free publicity from articles about his business in magazines, newspapers, and on television.

she told him to come up with his own idea, Jason settled on buglike pencil

On weekends, Jason works on Pencil Bugs. He makes hundreds at a time with some help from his parents. The bugs come in eight different colors. Each has its own certificate that notes the Pencil Bug's name and care and training instructions. When an order comes in, Jason packages and mails it. He admits that making the Pencil Bugs can take a lot of time and be repetitive. He hopes to **mass-produce** the Pencil Bugs in the future.

Jason has plans to grow his business. He wants to create Pencil Bugs video games, board games, and a children's book series. He hopes to make enough money to support himself when he is older. Currently he donates some of his proceeds to charity and plans to donate more in the future. For kids who want to get started in business, Jason thinks that being organized is important. He says that kids should have a plan because that is the key to getting things done.

Going Out of Business

Eventually you may decide that you no longer want to be in business. Maybe you have met your goals. You may have new interests. When this happens, you could have a younger brother or sister or another neighborhood kid take over your business. Then politely tell your customers that you are leaving the business. Introduce them to the new business owner. If no one wants to take over your business, you can send your customers to a similar business. After you close, you should prepare a final profit statement. You also may need to close any business bank accounts and file papers with your state. It is a good idea to talk to an adult about your business closing.

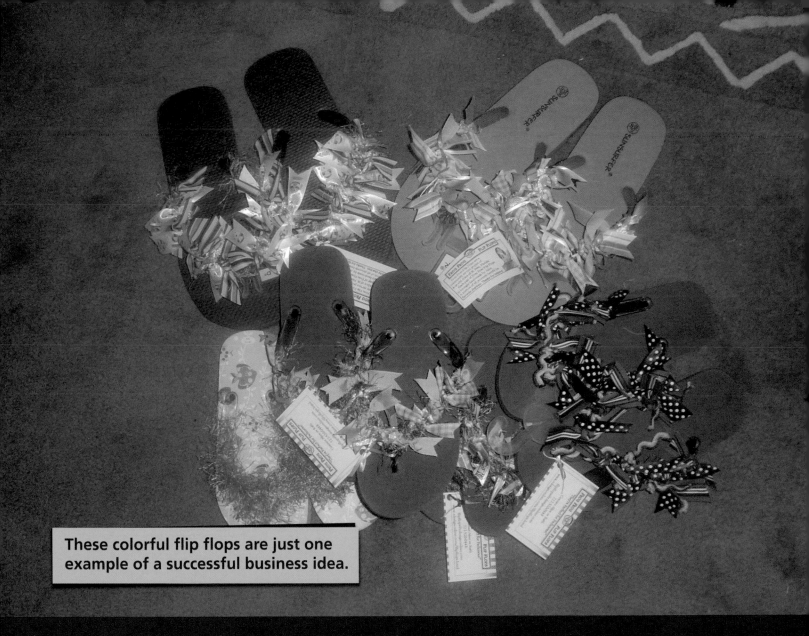

These colorful flip flops are just one example of a successful business idea.

Frou Frou Flip Flops

When Alice was in second grade, she learned about a tsunami that hit Southeast Asia. She wanted to raise money to help kids who had lost everything in the disaster. That year Alice had made a pair of decorated flip flops for Mother's Day. She thought they might be something she could turn into a business. Alice decided to name her business Frou Frou Flip Flops. To get started, Alice used her birthday money to buy supplies for her flip flops. Some people also gave her ribbon and flip-flop donations.

Alice says she gets ideas for her flip flops from the colors in her bedroom. She also says she gets design and color ideas when talking to people about their order. Sometimes she adds pieces

Alice started decorating flip flops like these when she was in second grade.

At 12 years old, Alice was still making flip flops.

like buttons and seashells to her flip flops. Alice makes most of the flip flops by herself, although her mom helps with gluing. Alice's mom also keeps spreadsheet records and helps with Alice's Web site.

Alice launched her Web site about four months after she started her business. Then most of her orders came through the site. She has found that word of mouth is the best form of advertising. People see other customers with her flip flops and want to know where they can get a pair. Articles about her business in magazines and newspapers have also spread the word about Frou Frou Flip Flops.

Alice donates most of her profits to charity. She chooses a different charity each quarter. Some of the charities that Alice has donated to include the American Cancer Society, the Make-A-Wish Foundation, and local animal protection societies.

Alice says that one of the hardest things about running her business is managing her time. Her parents insist that she only work on the business when it docs not interfere with school-work. She recommends that all kids considering starting a business think about their schedules first. She says that kids should make sure they have time for a business so that it does not become a chore.

Get Started

Hayleigh, Jason, and Alice are real-life examples of kids in business. They show that hard work and a little creativity go a long way in a successful business. By following their example, you can start a business doing something you enjoy. So go out there and try it!

Glossary

account balance (uh-KOUNT BAL-uhnss): The amount of money in a bank account at the end of the month or period.

accounts payable (uh-KOUNTZ PAY-a-buhl): Money that a business owes to its suppliers.

accounts receivable (uh-KOUNTZ ri-SEEV-a-buhl): Money that customers owe to a business.

advertising (AD-ver-tize-ing): Calling attention to a business and its products and services.

audiologist (aw-dee-OL-uh-jist): A doctor who studies and treats people with hearing disorders.

brainstorm (BRAYN-storm): Try to think up good ideas.

competition (kom-puh-TISH-uhn): Another person or business that is trying to reach the same customers.

deposits (di-POZ-itz): Money placed in a bank account.

evaluate (ee-VAL-you-ate): To examine and judge carefully.

expenses (ek-SPENS-uhz): Money paid to purchase supplies or pay employees.

feedback (FEED-bak): Information about a person's reaction to an object or activity.

income (IN-kuhm): Money received in payment for services or products.

interest (IN-trist): Money that a bank pays to account holders. It is usually calculated as a percentage of the account balance.

logo (LOH-goh): A graphic or symbol that represents a company.

mass-produce (mas-pruh-DOOS): To make in large quantities.

profitable (PROF-i-tuh-buhl): Making a profit, or money.

publicity (puh-BLISS-uh-tee): Information about a person or business that is spread in many ways to attract attention.

start-up costs (START-up kostz): Money you have to pay to start a business.

supplier (suh-PLYE-ur): A person or business who sells you supplies.

survey (SUR-vay): To gather information from a large group of people.

target market (TAR-git MAR-kit): The group of people that are most likely to buy the products or services of a business.

For More Information

Book

Bochner, Arthur. *The New Totally Awesome Business Book for Kids.* 3rd ed. New York: Newmarket, 2007.

Bernstein, Daryl. *Better Than A Lemonade Stand: Small Business Ideas for Kids.* Hillsboro, OR: Beyond Words Publishing, 1992.

Jones, Vada Lee. *Kids Can Make Money Too! How Young People Can Succeed Financially—Over 200 Ways to Earn Money and How to Make it Grow.* Menlo Park, CA: Calico Paws Publishing, 1987.

Rancic, Bill. *Beyond the Lemonade Stand.* New York: Razorbill, 2006.

Sember, Brette McWhorter. *The Everything Kids' Money Book: Earn It, Save It, and Watch It Grow!* Avon, MA: Adams Media, 2008.

Web Sites

Entrepreneur.com (www.entrepreneur.com/tsu/index.html). This Web site has a collection of articles for the young entrepreneur, including interviews, marketing tips, and business ideas.

Future Business Leaders of America (www.fbla-pbl.org). Future Business Leaders of America is a nonprofit education association for students preparing for careers in business. The association has several divisions, including one for middle school and junior high students.

Junior Achievement (www.ja.org). Junior Achievement educates students in grades kindergarten through 12th about business, entrepreneurship, and finance. The Web site's Student Center includes information on planning a business, money management, and business ethics.

MoneyInstructor.com (www.moneyinstructor.com) This Web site offers interactive lessons, articles and worksheets to teach kids about money skills, personal finance, money management, business, careers and more.

Teen Business Link (www.sba.gov/teens). This Web site, created by the U.S. Small Business Administration, offers information on the basics of starting a business and profiles of young entrepreneurs.

These Kids Mean Business (www.thesekidsmeanbusiness.org) Inspired by the PBS documentary *These Kids Mean Business,* this Web site features video clips, student profiles, essays, lesson plans, KidBiz games and links to entrepreneurship education programs.

Index

About the Author

Carla Mooney is the author of several books for young adults and children. She lives in Pittsburgh, Pennsylvania, with her husband and three children.